THE SIOUX

A First Americans Book

Virginia Driving Hawk Sneve

illustrated by Ronald Himler

Holiday House / New York

Text copyright © 1993 by Virginia Driving Hawk Sneve
Illustrations copyright © 1993 by Ronald Himler
All rights reserved
Printed in the United States of America
First Edition

Library of Congress Cataloging-in-Publication Data
Sneve, Virginia Driving Hawk.
The Sioux: a first Americans book / by Virginia Driving Hawk Sneve ; illustrated by Ronald Himler.
p.   cm.
Summary: Identifies the different tribes of the Sioux Indians and
discusses their beliefs and traditional way of life.
ISBN 0-8234-1017-X
1. Dakota Indians — Juvenile literature.   [1. Dakota Indians.
2. Indians of North America — Great Plains.]   I. Himler, Ronald, ill.   II. Title.
E99.D1S6277   1993   92-23946   CIP   AC
973′.04975 — dc20

NORTH DAKOTA

MINNESOTA

Lake Superior

YANKTONAIS

TETON (LAKOTA)

WISCONSIN

SOUTH DAKOTA

Lake Michigan

DAKOTA

YANKTON (NAKOTA)

NEBRASKA

IOWA

KANSAS

CREATION STORY

From birth to death the Indian revered his surroundings.
He considered himself born in the luxurious lap of Mother
Earth and no place was to him humble.

STANDING BEAR

They say that long ago the Great Spirit caused a hard rain that flooded the land. All of the people drowned except one girl who climbed to a high cliff. She lifted her arms to the sky and asked the Great Spirit to save her. As she prayed, an eagle swooped down, and the girl grabbed his legs.

The strong eagle carried the girl over the flooded land to the Black Hills. He landed on a high mountain and turned into a young man. The eagle man and the girl became parents, and so began the Dakota tribe.

MOVING TO THE PLAINS

*Great Spirit, bless Mother Earth so the people will live
in harmony with nature.*

HIGH BEAR

ceremonial pipe

The Dakota lived near lakes and in woods in what is now Minnesota, when white men met them in the 1600s. The women planted corn and squash, and the men fished and hunted woodland animals. But the arrival of white men changed the Dakota way of life. The white men traded their guns with the Dakota for furs. The Dakota used the guns to become better hunters and warriors.

The whites also brought the horse from Spain. Many horses escaped onto the Plains, where the Indian tribes found them. Because of the horse, the Dakota began to settle in the Plains in the 1700s. Part of them became the Lakota and Nakota tribes.

The name *Dakota* means allies or friends, but the French gave the name *Sioux* to the Dakota. The French got the name from the Ojibwa, who called their Dakota enemies *Nadewesiou*, "treacherous snake." *Sioux* is now the general name for the Dakota and related tribes.

bone flesher
(tool for scraping
buffalo hide)

On the Plains, the buffalo was the center of Sioux life. The men hunted and killed the buffalo and gave it to the women, who butchered it, wasting nothing. They made tipis, beds, blankets, moccasins, clothing, and robes from the hides. They made storage boxes from strong rawhide and used leather strips to lace the tipis together and to make bridles. Buffalo bones were used to make tools for farming, scraping, and sewing. In the winter the ribs were used as sleds.

Lakota box

Lakota parfleche (bag)

The buffalo was also the main food source of the Sioux. The women cooked the meat in a bowl they made by stretching the buffalo's stomach over a wooden frame. They filled the bowl with water that they heated with hot stones. The women dried the meat to eat in the winter. A favorite dish was *wasna* or pemmican. It was made by pounding dried meat and berries into fine bits and mixing them with suet. The Indians ate this tasty, nutritious food when the village moved or when the men went on a hunting trip.

The buffalo made the Sioux wealthy. After the white men came, the Sioux traded buffalo hides and beaver pelts for guns, iron kettles, calico, beads, and whiskey, thus becoming even wealthier.

VILLAGE LIFE

cradleboard

*What we consider the most important thing on earth
is our children.*

BEN BLACK BEAR

umbilical cord amulets *(The cord was placed
in a turtle-shaped leather case and worn
on a thong around a child's neck,
or placed in the tipi.)*

buckskin doll

All men had a say in making decisions for a village, but one highly respected man was the leader, or chief. Men had the most power. They could even have more than one wife. Though women did not play an active role in tribal government, a man's wives could persuade him to do what they thought was best for the people. Women owned everything in the family tipi, including the children.

Young boys and girls played together near their mothers. The boys pretended to hunt and fight with small bows and arrows. The girls played with buckskin dolls and tiny tipis.

When the boys and girls were five or six years old, they no longer played together. Older boys and men taught the boys to be hunters and warriors. The boys were taken along on a hunt or battle, where they took care of the horses and watched how the men hunted or fought.

The girls spent their time with the older girls and women. They learned how to cook, quill or bead, tan hides, and make moccasins and clothing. Both boys and girls were expected to care for younger brothers and sisters.

Children were not praised for doing something well, since they were expected always to do their best. When they did something wrong, they were often scolded loudly by each member of the family, instead of being spanked. Children did not like to be scolded in front of others, so they quickly learned the correct way to behave.

Everyone in the tribe loved children. Grandparents told them stories that taught proper behavior or tribal and family history. When food was scarce, the children were fed first. During a battle, adults would shield children with their bodies.

THE CIRCLE OF LIFE

The moon, the horizon, the rainbow — circles within circles,
with no beginning and no end.

LAME DEER

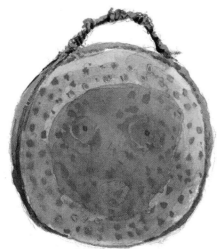

hand drum

The Sioux believed that the Great Spirit created a circle of life on earth. In that circle, the Great Spirit caused the buffalo and all creatures and things to come from the earth. The Sioux called the earth "mother." They believed they were related to all creatures and things on Earth. Every time the Sioux cut a tree for a tipi pole, or caught a fish, or killed game, they thanked the spirits for giving up a life so that the people could live. The Sioux believed that they must take care of each other as well as the earth and everything on it.

The Sioux had many rituals and ceremonies. A young man went on a vision quest after a sweat-bath ceremony. The steam in the bath was so hot, it made him sweat and cleansed his body while he prayed and concentrated on good thoughts. The vision was sent by the Great Spirit to serve as a guide throughout the man's life.

A medicine man led the special ceremonies of the sweat bath, healed the sick, found lost people or objects, and directed the Sun Dance.

Brave young men performed the Sun Dance after a successful hunt, battle, or if a loved one had recovered from an illness.

During the Sun Dance, a man was tied to a center pole by a leather thong on his breast. As he stared at the sun, he fasted, prayed, and danced until the leather thong broke.

eagle-feather headdress

Men wore single eagle feathers in their hair or in a headdress so that they would have the bird's strength and courage, and the favor of the Great Spirit. The eagle was sacred because it was the strongest and bravest of all birds. The eagle-feather headdress was worn only for special occasions. The men of several tribes wore it when they gathered for the Sun Dance, or in meetings held with white men to discuss treaties. Today, the headdress is still worn at tribal meetings and ceremonies.

Girls and women did not seek visions, but later, after they had grandchildren, they could become medicine women and do the same things as the medicine man. A medicine woman often was more skilled than a man in using plants to heal wounds and cure illness. Females also had their own special sweat ceremonies.

IN BATTLE

If you try to do something and you fail, keep trying.

FOOLS CROW

war club

Even though the Sioux had enemies like the Ojibwa, they fought their main battles while raiding horses from other tribes. A man was meant to be a brave warrior, but so were some women. A good warrior was not afraid to die in battle.

The Sioux were brave, but they were no match for white men's diseases and guns. Diseases like smallpox were new to the Sioux, and many died from them. The white men also killed so many buffalo that there were none left for the Sioux to hunt, and many Sioux died from hunger.

THE SIOUX TODAY

One does not sell the earth upon which the people walk.
CRAZY HORSE

**Bear Butte, a sacred site in the
Black Hills of South Dakota**

The Sioux had wise leaders. Sitting Bull and Crazy Horse were two of the men who led their people to defeat General Custer at the Battle of the Little Bighorn in 1876. It was a great victory for the Sioux, but after the battle the Army forced the Indians to go to the reservations.

Buffalo Bill persuaded Sitting Bull and other Sioux warriors to join his Wild West show. Sitting Bull didn't like the way the show made a spectacle of the Sioux, and he returned. He advised his people to "pick up what is good from the white man's path, but if it is bad, throw it away."

Today on reservations in South Dakota, North Dakota, Montana, and Minnesota, the Sioux try to follow Sitting Bull's advice. There are many Sioux who live in cities and towns and still treasure their Sioux heritage.

TRIBES OF THE SIOUX

The Eastern Dakota was the mother tribe, which split into three major groups as the Dakota moved west. Each group has its own dialect. For example, the Dakota pronounce the Sioux word for "thank you" *pidamiye*, while the Nakota say *pinamiye*, and the Lakota say *pilamiye*.

	DAKOTA	
Dakota	*Yankton* *or* *Nakota*	*Teton* *or* *Lakota*
Mdewakanton	Yankton	Sicangu (Brule)
Wahpekute	Yanktonais	Oglala
Wahpeton		Hunkpapa
Sisseton		Minneconjou
		Sihasapa (Blackfeet)
		Oohenumpa (Two Kettle)
		Itazipo (Sans Arc)

From the Lakota Pipe Ceremony

Red is the east.
It is where the daybreak star,
The star of knowledge appears.
Red is the rising sun
Bringing us a new day.

The south is yellow.
Our Mother Earth gives us our growth.
She brings forth the bounty of springtime
From the warm south wind.

Black is the color of the west
Where the sun goes down.
Black is darkness, release, spirit protection.
In the darkness, the spirit beings come to us.

White is for the north.
Strength, endurance, purity, truth
Stand for the north.
The north covers our Mother Earth
With the white blanket of cleansing snow.

Father Sky gives energy from the sun.
Father Sky provides the fire that
Warms our lodges
And the energy that moves our bodies.

Green is the color for Mother Earth.
Every part of us comes from her
Through the food we daily take from her.
We all start as tiny seeds.
We have grown through what she provides.

Great Spirit, Creator of us all,
Creator of the four directions,
Creator of our Mother Earth and Father Sky
And all related things,
We offer this pipe.

INDEX